THE PENTHOUSE BLUEPRINT

THE PENTHOUSE BLUEPRINT

COLLECTION

VIKKI JONES

The publisher is not responsible for websites, online platforms, or social media content related to this work that are not officially managed by the publisher.

Paperback ISBN: 979-8-99-183612-8

Publisher Disclaimer:
The content in this publication reflects the lived experiences, personal reflections, and professional insights of the author. Any views, interpretations, or observations expressed are solely those of the author and are not intended to represent advice, guarantees, or endorsements by the publisher. Readers are encouraged to reflect, interpret, and apply the material in a way that aligns with their own journey and discernment. The publisher disclaims any liability for actions taken based on this content.

Published in the United States of America

10 9 8 7 6 5 4 3 2 1

VMH™ Publishing
Atlanta | New York | Worldwide

Preface

There's something deeply unsettling about being boxed into an identity that doesn't reflect your truth. For years, people tried to shape me into who they thought I should be—safe, predictable, palatable. It served them. But it suffocated me.

So I broke away. Not recklessly, but intentionally. And in doing so, I started noticing something. Every time I followed my intuition and stood in my own vision, the world shifted in response.

I wasn't just getting invited—I was being positioned. Repeatedly, I found myself in spaces reserved for the elite: penthouses, international summits, exclusive gatherings with world leaders, athletes, royalty, creators, visionaries.

One moment stands out. I was simply waiting for my car after an event. I decided to stroll—nothing more. Someone I didn't know told me to enjoy some refreshments while I waited and escorted me to a private elevator.
"You're going to the penthouse," they said.
I assumed others were too.
But no—it was just for me.

Inside: Luxury. Stillness. Power. Intention.

That moment—and many others like it—confirmed something I already sensed: My life is aligning with a vision greater than I imagined.

I'm not forcing my way into rooms. The doors are opening because I've finally stepped into who I was always meant to be.

Introduction

———— •◆• ————

Welcome to *The Penthouse Blueprint: Collection.*

This isn't just a book. It's a rhythm. A resonance. A real-time frequency shift— captured, lived, and documented.

Inside these pages is proof that alignment isn't a buzzword. It's a lived reality. One you can feel. One you've likely already tasted— even if you haven't fully named it yet.

This is not about striving. It's about seeing. Seeing what's already unfolding around you... and within you. You're not trying to arrive— you're remembering that you're already here.

The stories in this book aren't just chapters. They're activations. Each one is a turning point—an intuitive nudge, a moment of clarity, a divine confirmation.

Not of effort, but of embodiment. You're not chasing anymore. You're choosing.

And what you're choosing now—your presence, your peace, your position—carries more influence than anything you've ever had to prove.

This is the architecture of a shift. A life lived above the noise. Where you stop explaining your value and start embodying it. Where you stop trying to get in the room—and realize the room is already watching.

The rhythm of your next level is already within you. This book simply helps you stay tuned to it.

*"I didn't chase the room. I aligned with the rhythm.
And once I did, the doors—those I never knocked on—
swung open. Not because I arrived.
But because I remembered who I was."*

— Vikki Jones

The Penthouse Blueprint: Collection

Table of Contents

The Penthouse Moment — Ushered Into Alignment

———— ••• ————

I wasn't looking for anything.

No expectation, no search for connection. I wasn't trying to be noticed. I keep to myself—but I love people, so I speak. I smile. I'm warm, but I don't force moments.

That evening, I was standing outside after a high-level event, waiting for valet to bring my car. The crowd had thinned, conversations were soft, and the energy in the air had calmed. There was stillness. A natural exhale after an elevated room has emptied.

Just a few feet from where I stood was a balcony that overlooked the ocean. Below, people were enjoying the pool. It was a peaceful view— elevated, open, expansive. I walked over to take it in. I pulled out my phone and began recording the tide, the rhythm of the water. But nearby, a group of people were having a conversation and seemed to think I was recording them. I wasn't—I was focused on the ocean. Still, to avoid any unnecessary tension, I decided to walk away and explore another area of the venue.

I rounded the corner, following signs to another section of the conference. I wasn't in a rush, but with only about twenty minutes left before valet retrieved my car, I realized it would take too long to get there. So I started to turn back.

And that's when it happened.

Someone standing near the entrance of a private event looked over and saw me. Not like a quick glance or background acknowledgment. They saw me. Like there was a quiet recognition. A sense of knowing.

Then they said, with calm certainty:
"You should enjoy some refreshments."

No questions. No credentials. Just direction.

I walked over near her, and she guided me to the elevator. As the door opened, she personally reached inside, pressed the button, and said,
"You're going to the penthouse."

I paused.

Others were in the elevator heading to their rooms, so I assumed we were all going up together. But I was wrong.

This wasn't about all.
This was about me.

When I stepped off, I immediately felt it. The space was quiet and elevated. Great lighting. A refined group of people. A layout that whispered intention. Refreshments arranged thoughtfully. And past the glass windows: the ocean—endless and still.

I left my bag at the entrance and stepped onto the balcony.

Then my phone died.
No big deal—I had a backup charger.

It died too. Fully charged. No explanation. But instead of frustration, I took it as a signal:

This moment is not for documentation.
It's for embodiment.
It's for you.

So I leaned into it. Fully present.
Two pastries. Two bottles of water. A view that felt like clarity.
A room that didn't ask for anything but presence.

I hadn't asked for any of this.
And yet, here I was—in a penthouse I didn't seek out.
Directed by someone I didn't know.
Standing in a space that felt... designed for me.

And it wasn't the first time.

There have been moments—often unexpected—when I've been shifted from what I chose into something far more elevated. Booked one hotel, got sent to a more luxurious suite. Reserved something solid, ended up in something spectacular. Not because I asked. But because the moment carried me there.

And recently, I'd been thinking about buying a home. Nothing grand. Just something good.

But that night, I stood in a penthouse.
I hadn't asked.
I hadn't pitched.
I simply followed the moment.
And it found me.

That's when I understood:

This wasn't just about the view.
It was about the placement.

It was a reminder of how often I've been gently guided into something greater—quietly, precisely, effortlessly.

It wasn't about luxury.
It was about alignment.

That moment—standing there, no phone, no distractions, just stillness—marked something in me.

It became the confirmation.
I knew this book had to be written.

Not because I needed to prove anything.
But because it's been happening over and over again.
And this time, I wasn't going to explain it away.

No name-dropping.
No striving.
Just presence.
Just alignment.
Just truth.

Because this level keeps finding me.
Not because I chase it.
But because I've been flowing in it—quietly, consistently, unshakably.

And I'm done downplaying that.

This is who I am.
This is the blueprint I've been aligned with.
And now, I understand what that really means.

Penthouse Decoding:

This wasn't just a moment.
It was a message.

The penthouse wasn't about status.
It was about identity.
A visual confirmation of what's been evolving internally.
A reset of standard.

A reminder that what's for you doesn't need to be chased.

This wasn't about striving.
It was alignment in motion.

When you're met with the best—without angling for it—it's not ego.
It's evidence.

Evidence that you've moved into something bigger than strategy.
You've been becoming.
And now the space is responding.

Reflection Point

- Where have I been settling for good when alignment was offering something better?

- What experiences have matched what I didn't even think to ask for?

- Have I honored those moments—or tried to shrink them down to logic?

Activation Cue

Start preparing for the level that keeps choosing you.

Not the one you feel safe requesting.

The one you're already living in.

Why I Wrote This Book

———— ⋅♦⋅ ————

That evening was the confirmation—but the story had been writing itself long before then.

I wrote this because I felt an urge—an importance, almost a sense of vitality—to document it.

There were things I could not ignore—what had been unfolding in front of me for some time. These unfoldings had been happening for a long time, but I didn't see it as I see it now. I think I see it the way I see it because the pace of it has sped up.

There were too many moments—unexpected, undeniable, unforced—when I found myself in elevated spaces I never planned to enter.

I didn't scheme.

I didn't pitch.

I simply followed alignment.

And alignment led me to rooms, relationships, revelations, and realities that exceeded what I had ever thought to ask for.

This book captures a few of those moments.

It's a collection of real stories, sharp turns, quiet

truths, and divine confirmations—all of which revealed themselves within a short, concentrated period of time.

From elite introductions and global business events to spontaneous opportunities and sacred nudges to open doors—the thread between them all was this:

I wasn't chasing.

I was being placed.

This isn't a book about luxury.

It's about alignment.

It's about recognizing when you've shifted frequencies—and how your life begins responding to that shift.

It's for the ones who've been rising without applause.

Who've been guided without explanation.

Who've been elevated—quietly, consistently—and are just now starting to realize:

You're not "on the way."

You're already there.

I wrote this book to help you accept what you already know deep down.

To accept growth.

And to accept what must happen as you begin to embrace more of yourself.

The shedding.

The becoming.

The moments when the best life has to offer reveals itself—and your only responsibility is to receive it without shrinking.

So I wrote this book as both a mirror and a message.

To name what's been happening.

To honor what I once tried to minimize.

To help others see what alignment looks like—when it's real, when it's divine, and when it requires no performance.

This is *The Penthouse*.

And it's been waiting for you, too.

Chapter 1

The Truth About Intentions

There came a point in my life when I realized:

if I wanted better, I had to choose better.

Not just long for it. Not just wish for it.

Choose it—with my time, my presence, my relationships, my money, my energy.

I had to be intentional.

About everything.

I stopped waiting for the right people to find me.

I started placing myself—physically and mentally —where I knew I belonged.

Even when I was scared. Even when the environment felt unfamiliar.

I moved anyway.

Because alignment doesn't arrive at your doorstep —you meet it halfway.

So I packed my bags and flew across continents.

But this wasn't aimless.

I had already been confirmed as a speaker—secured a place on a global stage I never would've reached had I not stretched.

And I mean really stretched.

Beyond convenience.

Beyond comfort.

I pushed myself with one goal in mind:

to meet the version of me that refused to settle.

I didn't show up for validation.

I showed up because I needed to know what it felt like to be valued— not for what I could do, but for who I am.

And that required courage.

It required intention.

And it required a refusal to accept anything less than my best.

This wasn't about proving anything to anyone else. It was about being relentless in what I knew I deserved.

I couldn't keep shrinking.

Couldn't keep settling for friendships that only showed up when I was useful,

or partnerships that only worked if I played small.

I was tired of being tolerated when I was built to thrive.

So I made a decision:

To go after environments that saw my full worth.

To connect with people who weren't intimidated by my light.

To build relationships rooted in mutual respect— not convenience.

To stop explaining myself and start elevating myself.

Yes, some of the people I left behind were kind.

Familiar.

Maybe even supportive in their own way.

But if their presence came at the cost of my peace, my growth, or my progress,

I had to choose me.

That was the truth about intention.

My intention.

I became more aware—of what I had been allowing, accepting, and tolerating.

And once I turned that awareness inward, everything started to shift.

I asked myself the hard questions:

Why am I still in this space?

Does this serve the version of me I'm becoming?

What am I saying "yes" to that's really a quiet "no" to myself?

And once I answered those questions honestly, I couldn't unsee the truth.

I became intentional with my time—only showing up where I felt seen.

Intentional with my presence—reserving it for places that didn't require me to shrink.

Intentional with my energy—protecting it from anything that pulled me backwards.

And something shifted.

The environments changed.

The people changed.

The doors opened faster—but not because I forced them.

Because I was finally walking in the direction they were waiting in.

There were moments that tested me.

Nights alone in hotel rooms halfway across the world,

wondering if I'd done too much, reached too far.

But every time I leaned into discomfort, I was met with clarity.

Courage doesn't mean you're not afraid.

It means you refuse to let fear make your choices.

So no, this chapter isn't about what others intended for me.

It's about what I intended for myself.

To be surrounded by excellence.

To build a life that reflects my worth.

To never again mistake usefulness for love.

To rise—fully, freely, and without apology.

That's the real truth about intentions.

When your intention is clear, your elevation is non-negotiable.

Penthouse Decoding:

You don't need to explain why you chose yourself.

You don't owe anyone an apology for outgrowing what no longer fits.

And you certainly don't need permission to go after what you deserve.

Intentionality is power.

It moves you beyond wishful thinking and into alignment.

Let your actions reflect what you know you're

worthy of.

Reflection Point

• Where in my life have I accepted less than I truly deserved?

• What decisions am I avoiding that could elevate me?

• What does self-honoring intentionality look like in this season?

Activation Cue

You don't have to wait for the world to affirm your value.

Choose you.

Stretch.

Move with courage—your rhythm will catch up.

Chapter 2

No Gate, No Panic — Just Precision

Some shifts don't look like alignment at first.
They look like delays.
They feel like inconvenience.
But the blueprint is still being built—often in silence, and always on time.

I wasn't running late.
I was exactly on schedule for the version of me that would arrive with clarity, confidence, and favor.

Lightning struck in Chicago. I didn't see it from the terminal, but I felt the consequences. Flights slowed. Air traffic control made decisions the rest of us couldn't hear. Still, I felt at ease—calm, focused, and fully on my way to Thailand.

I was headed to Bangkok to serve as a moderator for one of the featured sessions at the largest fintech conference in the world—an event held in four continents annually. This wasn't a casual speaking engagement. It was a defining one. A door-opening moment. And I was determined to arrive ready.

Then the phone rang. Not my email. Not a boarding announcement. My actual phone. It was the gate agent. He asked me to come confirm my passport and travel details. Unusual, but I complied. He was polite, almost overly intentional. He printed all the tickets I'd need and made sure my seat was one I'd appreciate. I walked away thinking, Wow. That was smooth.

What I didn't realize at the time was that my connecting gate from Hong Kong to Thailand hadn't been printed on the ticket. I didn't think to check—I assumed everything I needed was already in hand. For reasons I still can't explain, I genuinely thought I was fully prepared.

We finally boarded, and the delay in Chicago faded behind me. I ended up in a nearly empty row, just one other person seated on the far end. That small pocket of space felt like a reset button. I rested, journaled, took mental notes, and landed in Hong Kong with a calm sense of focus.

The plan was to connect quickly, grab my next gate, and head straight to Thailand. My layover was supposed to be short—a little over an hour— but the lightning delay had taken a slice out of it. Still, I moved confidently through the airport, walking briskly with all my essentials in hand.

But the closer I got to the gate I thought was mine, the quieter things became. No chatter. No lines. No announcements. Something felt off.

I looked down at my ticket again, and that's when it hit me.

What I'd been reading as my gate number... was my seat number. I had no gate. No idea where to go.

And yet, I didn't panic. I didn't freeze. I just moved. Fast, but clear.

I found the nearest customer service counter and explained the situation. They typed rapidly, checked the system, and gently let me know: my flight had just closed its doors. The plane was preparing for takeoff. They even radioed the aircraft to see if I could board—but it was too late.

Then something shifted again.

The agent called someone. I could hear her voice, but I couldn't understand—she was speaking in another language to her colleague. Still, her kindness and determination to help were unmistakable. Then she turned to me and said gently, "Go to the airline's main service desk. They're expecting you."

I walked fast. When I arrived, someone was standing there—not holding a paper with my name, just a quiet sign, as if waiting for someone who needed it. That someone was me.

And that's when the blueprint started revealing itself.

Without hesitation, they rebooked me on a flight for the following morning—giving me more than enough time to make my event. They arranged a room in a hotel directly connected to the airport. No shuttles. No confusion. Just convenience, comfort, and quiet. They handed me a meal voucher and reminded me that everything was covered.

That night, I rested well. I didn't even use the voucher until the next morning—the airline food had been more than enough. Instead, I took a long, hot shower, unpacked just enough to feel settled, and sat for a moment in stillness. I reflected. I regrouped. I didn't rush to "fix" anything. I let it all unfold.

Ironically, had I booked a hotel in Bangkok in advance, I would have arrived at almost the exact same time—rushed, uncertain, and potentially stressed. But because I hadn't, I was exactly where I needed to be.

No panic. No need to fix it. Just alignment—
revealed through a closed gate.

Penthouse Decoding:

Some alignments only make sense in hindsight.
They don't arrive with spotlights or certainty—
sometimes, they arrive in silence. Through delays.
Through closed doors. Through what feels like
missed moments.

But alignment doesn't miss.
It recalibrates.

What looked like a missed flight was actually a
mapped pause. A precise reset. A moment carved
out for restoration I didn't know I would need—
because clarity doesn't always wait until you land.
Sometimes, it greets you when the door won't
open.

The real shift wasn't in the rebooking.
It was in the way I responded.
No panic. No pressure. Just presence.

That's how you know alignment is active:

when your peace doesn't leave just because the plan did.

Everything I needed was waiting.
Not because I demanded it—but because I was willing to move without fear when the blueprint shifted.

Because had everything gone according to my schedule, I would've arrived flustered and rushed.
But instead, I arrived composed, clear, and centered—on time for the version of me that was meant to show up.

The blueprint wasn't broken.
It was unfolding.

Reflection Point

• Have you ever mistaken a disruption for a detour, when it was actually a redirect?
• How often do you leave room for things to work themselves out without your control?
• What details have you tried to micromanage that may actually work better if you release them?

Activation Cue

Instead of forcing your way through what's

closing, ask this:

"What's waiting to meet me on the other side of letting go?"

Chapter 3

The Signature — When Worlds Quietly Collide

———————

I came to the fintech conference in Asia to moderate my panel. That was the assignment. But something told me to look deeper into the agenda —like there was something more I was meant to take in.

That's when I saw the AI panel. It aligned with the broader theme of technology and finance and was set on one of the largest stages. The speakers were from different nations, each with impressive résumés, and I felt drawn to the discussion.

As I took my seat, the conversation quickly engaged the room. Insightful. Future-forward. Well delivered. But then something began to bother me—not on the surface, but underneath. One of the panelists kept drawing comparisons between his country and mine. Repeatedly.

It wasn't framed negatively. It wasn't even combative. It was prideful—an assertion of how far, how fast, and how powerfully his country was moving on the global AI stage. He didn't just say it once. He said it again and again.

I shifted in my seat.

The timing of it all felt ironic. As he spoke, the global economy was going through a visible shift. Large and small businesses across continents were adjusting to it. And both of our nations were involved in that shift in deeply complicated ways.

I wasn't angry. Just uncomfortable. I didn't cross an ocean to be reminded—repeatedly—of a comparison I didn't ask for. So I left. Midway through. And I returned to the VIP Lounge.

I sat in silence for a while, still unsettled, and eventually got up to walk.

As I stepped out, I saw them—three of the speakers from the panel—seated near the front of the VIP Lounge. They hadn't seen me, but I saw them. And something in me said, Don't walk past this moment.

I approached them directly and said, "I caught part of your panel on AI—it was a strong conversation." Then I paused and continued, "I left midway through, though, and I'd like to share why."

I didn't want to dive into politics, and I certainly wasn't looking for conflict. But I also couldn't ignore what I'd felt.

I told them plainly: I hadn't traveled across the world to absorb subtle rankings between nations —especially when we were all there as contributors, not competitors. The truth is, anyone paying attention to the global landscape at that time knew exactly how sensitive the political climate was. So hearing repeated comparisons— however well-intended—landed differently.

I was honest. Not combative. Just clear. And to their credit, they listened.

The conversation shifted from global positioning to personal purpose.

We began discussing our respective work. Our companies. Our projects. I showed them my Instagram to offer a glimpse of what I do, and one of them paused as he saw a familiar face— someone I had taken a photo with and posted long ago.

It was him: the founder of the trillion-dollar AI chip empire. The global tech giant whose name shapes the industry. I had met him at a conference in Los Angeles. I remembered the moment clearly.

He didn't just shake hands and move on—he took the time to listen. And I made sure to thank him. I told him that his work helped my company match the speed at which I work. That what he built enabled my systems and workflows to perform at the same level of excellence and precision that I demand. He was kind. Present. Sincere.

That's also why I admire him so deeply—not just for the empire he built, but for how he built it. He started his journey as a boy who had moved from Asia to America. He washed dishes in a restaurant while holding on to the dreams that most people would have dismissed. But he didn't give up. And years later, after quietly creating the foundation for supercomputing chips, his company exploded into the stratosphere. The world caught up to his vision.

So yes, I admire him. For his brilliance, his humility, and his perseverance.

Back in the VIP Lounge, the panelist who saw my photo lit up. "Wait," he said, pulling out his own photo with the same tech visionary. Then, he reached into his bag and pulled out a book. The same founder had signed it the year before. "He signed it here," he said proudly. "I met him while I was living in America."

Then came the twist.

He pulled out a second copy of the book—what appeared to be a journal—and handed it to me.

"Would you sign this one?" he asked. "Right here. Just like he did."

I froze, unsure of what to say. I'm not a billionaire. I'm not world-famous. I flew in for a single panel. But I could tell this moment meant something to him. Somehow, my presence had registered with the same gravity as that of a global icon.

So I signed it.

The entire experience was strange—beautiful, humbling, and still confusing to this day. I don't know what he saw in me that made him ask. I don't know what future moment he was placing his belief in. But I didn't take it lightly.

As I handed the journal back to him, he looked at me and said, "Next time you see him"—referring to the tech visionary—"tell him I said hello."

It was unexpected. I hadn't asked for it, but the moment spoke louder than any applause could have. In that brief exchange, what started as discomfort had somehow turned into mutual respect.

The next day, we crossed paths again in the VIP Lounge. This time, he looked slightly distressed—he couldn't find his badge, and the lounge staff wasn't sure if he was supposed to be there. Without hesitation, I stepped in: "He's a speaker. I watched his panel. Here—these are the photos I took from his session." I vouched for him without thinking twice.

That's the part that still lingers.

What was this encounter really about?

It wasn't about the signature. Not really. It was about recognition. About shared presence in a world that's not as big as it sometimes feels. Somehow, one photograph and one mutual connection narrowed the globe—and eased the discomfort I had carried just moments before.

But even now, I wonder: What about me made him ask?

He had an impressive résumé. A man who had lived and worked within globally recognized tech companies. He lived in Washington, D.C.—not some casual attendee, but someone deeply familiar with prestige, intelligence, and power. He had already secured a signature from one of the most influential tech figures in the world. So why mine?

I wasn't a celebrity. I didn't hold a trillion-dollar valuation. I had simply shown up as myself—grounded, intentional, clear about who I am and what I represent. Maybe that was the difference.

Maybe he saw someone who wasn't trying to be important, but simply was.

Maybe he recognized the posture of purpose.

Or maybe—without knowing my full story—he still felt the gravity of it.

And that's what shook me most: the realization that people can see your imprint long before they understand your journey.

One of the speakers looked at me and said, "You have a way of drawing people to you."

I didn't quite know how to respond to that.

Because from where I stand, I still don't fully see what they see.

They don't know what my bank account looks like. They've never seen my balance sheets, my expenditures, or my asset portfolio. If they had, they might wonder how someone without the external benchmarks of wealth or widespread recognition could hold that kind of space.

But somehow, even without all the traditional signs of success, something about my presence speaks first.

It draws people in. It earns quiet respect. It unlocks doors I didn't pitch for.

And I've come to realize—it's not because of what I *have*.

It's because of who I *am*.

What they feel is alignment. And what I carry isn't loud—but it's undeniable.

Penthouse Decoding:

Sometimes your presence speaks before you do. It's not your title. It's not your credentials. It's the way you enter a room with clarity. The way you hold your silence with purpose. The way you navigate with intention and treat people with respect—even when the space around you feels unfamiliar or nuanced.

This chapter wasn't about a book signing. It was about alignment.

When someone who's already connected to global power asks you for your signature, it's not because they see you as aspiring. It's because—on some level—they see you as established. Positioned. Equal in essence, even if not yet in scale.

Even if you couldn't immediately understand why it happened, it was a moment of reflection. A mirror, not for who you hope to become, but for who you already are.

Reflection Point

- What are you carrying that others can sense—before you ever speak about it?
- Are you fully aware of how clearly your purpose shows up in the spaces you walk into?
- Have you ever paused to consider that a moment of honor was simply confirmation—not coincidence?

- How might your posture, presence, and precision be telling a story others deeply respect—even if they don't yet know your full name?
- What does it mean to move through elite environments with quiet certainty, knowing you belong?

Activation Cue

Write about a moment when someone acknowledged your value in a way you didn't expect.

Where were you?
How did you respond?
Did you downplay it—or let it shift something in you?
What would it look like to own that moment now?

Chapter 4

When Purpose Meets Precision

———————•———————

Purpose prepares the path, but precision unlocks the placement.

There are moments when life requires more than strategy—it requires you to lean in.
Not the kind of leaning in that suggests striving or force.
But the kind that lets go of how it's going to happen and trusts yourself enough to move—
with clarity, with courage, and with full commitment.

Less than two weeks ago, I did just that.

I gave everything.
Energy.
Intention.
Resources.
Time.

I didn't just travel—I moved with purpose.

I charted a path across continents not for leisure, not for luxury, but because I knew something sacred was unfolding. I was stepping into the version of myself that I had already seen—but hadn't yet fully met. The version of me who operated at the highest level. Who walked in rooms built for visionaries. Who didn't need to be chosen—because she had already accepted her own calling.

It wasn't a vacation. It was a mission.

The journey began in Florida. I had already mapped out the itinerary in full—every leg of the trip planned not just for where I needed to be, but for how I needed to feel when I arrived. I don't move chaotically. I move strategically. Every detail was accounted for—sleep, rest, decompression, transitions, ground transport. I ensured that my energy could remain high by honoring it before I ever boarded a flight.

Around that same time—just as I was finalizing logistics for this multi-stop journey—I received a last-minute speaking request. It was an invitation to lead a session on writing and publishing. The timing felt tight. The journey ahead was packed. But I recognized the alignment. The request wasn't random. It was confirmation that even before I left, the work was already making space for me. I accepted.

From there, the mission was activated.

I flew out of Florida and into Chicago. Then across the ocean to Hong Kong. From Hong Kong to Bangkok, Thailand.

I didn't go because it was easy or glamorous.
I went because I asked one clear, unsettling question:
Where do I need to be to rise into the next level of who I am?

The answer came quickly:
The Asian fintech conference..

Not just the event. Not just the location.
The frequency.

The level of dialogue. The standard of excellence.
The expectation of delivery.
That's where I belonged.

From the outside, it probably looked like an ambitious travel itinerary.
But no one saw what was happening internally.
I wasn't chasing opportunity.
I was walking into it—fully aware, fully prepared, and fully aligned.

Every appearance, every mile, every time zone—I moved as a strategist.
This wasn't burnout culture. This was blueprint execution.

I had calculated it all—right down to decompression hours, rest cycles, and reset pockets between major stages and transitions.

This wasn't about endurance.

It was about intelligence.

I don't wait to arrive before I prepare.

I prepare because I know where I'm going.

While in Bangkok, I received another invitation.

This time, from a company in London asking me to speak.

The topic was right. The platform was aligned.

But the timing—4 a.m. Thailand time—wasn't.

I considered it. Tried to make the schedule work.

But I knew immediately:

That wasn't my moment.

I didn't decline because I couldn't handle it.

I declined because my precision told me where my energy was most needed.

That's what this journey had taught me.

Every "yes" has weight.

And when you're fully aligned, you don't dilute your impact trying to be everywhere.

As the Bangkok engagement wrapped, the next leg of the journey began.

I flew from Bangkok to Tokyo. Then Tokyo to Chicago.

No hotel. No downtime.
I drove straight to Green Bay, Wisconsin.

Why?
Because I had a room to be in. A message to deliver.
A moment to honor.

From Green Bay, I returned to Florida—landing in Orlando—and then made not one, but two separate drives to Miami for back-to-back appearances.

Each one with intention.
Each one with clarity.
Each one anchored by the decision to show up fully, no matter the schedule.

These weren't soft landings.
These were power placements—executed within a seven-day window.

There was no chaos. No fatigue.
Only purpose.
And precision.

Penthouse Decoding:

Purpose prepares the path, but precision unlocks the placement.

Some journeys aren't about how far you travel, but how clearly you move in alignment with who you are becoming. Purpose gives you the assignment, but it's precision that helps you complete it—and completing it well requires more than just organization. It requires discernment. It requires knowing where your presence holds weight and honoring that with every step.

Without alignment, even the most ambitious strategies become noise. You can be in motion and still be misaligned. Precision is what transforms that motion into meaningful momentum. It makes the difference between showing up just to be seen—and showing up because you've been sent.

Preparation isn't about control. It's about protection. It's how you shield your energy so your delivery stays powerful, even under pressure. That's what makes the blueprint sustainable—it's not just the vision, it's how you honor the vessel that carries it.

And here's what most people miss: you don't always need a spotlight to validate your worth. True precision often places you in rooms where your presence alone shifts the atmosphere. No announcement. No introduction. Just alignment—and undeniable impact.

Reflection Point

- Purpose will give you the assignment, but precision will help you complete it.

- Strategy without alignment is just movement —only precision makes that movement meaningful.

- Preparation is less about controlling every detail and more about protecting the energy that powers your delivery.

- When you're truly aligned, the spaces you enter don't require a performance—your presence alone speaks volumes.

Activation Cue

Where in your life have you been delaying your next move in the name of "getting ready"? What if your readiness isn't about doing more—but deciding faster? Identify one area where you've already received clarity. Now define the next precise move you need to make—and give it a deadline.

Chapter 5

The Stories Found Me

———————•———————

It was a whirlwind—but not chaotic. Every leg of the journey was mapped out with intention. I didn't just travel—I moved with precision so I could be fully present for every assignment along the way.

After my talk in Bangkok, I flew to Tokyo, landed in Denver, and then made my way to Chicago. From there, I rented a car and drove three hours to Green Bay, Wisconsin. I didn't know what the drive would look like. The route was unfamiliar. But I knew I had to take it to complete everything I had mapped out across what began as a seven-day itinerary—and extended into ten. Green Bay wasn't the end. I still had two more events ahead in Miami.

But first—this.

Before arriving in Green Bay, I already knew I had a webinar scheduled. Not a maybe. Not a "see how things go." It was already set.

So I found a quiet space, created a setup that worked, and honored my word.

It wasn't haphazard. It was part of the plan.

And in that tucked-away corner of stillness, I showed up.

The topic? Writing and publishing real stories. But what I shared went far beyond technique.

I talked about why your story matters—why it's worth documenting while you're still living it. I walked through professional insights on publishing, creative marketing strategies, and practical ways to sell your book with clarity and confidence.

I also shared something I believe deeply: most people don't even realize they're walking around with money in them—their story. I told them how writing changed my life. How becoming a publisher didn't start with prestige—it started with pain, with purpose, with realizing that what I had lived through wasn't just for me. That story became a bridge. It opened doors I never knew existed. It helped me heal, and it helped others do the same. That's what publishing can do. It's not just ink on paper—it's legacy in motion.

I enjoyed every moment. The exchange was honest, meaningful, and free from pressure. I wasn't performing. I was just telling the truth.

And right in the middle of that live session—something shifted.

An email came through. Someone watching said they wanted to work with me. Not later—now. By the time I signed off, another person said they were finally ready to write their story. And before I could even gather my notes, a third emailed—ready to publish their manuscript.

These weren't compliments. These weren't vague ideas. They were commitments. Real people. Real stories. Ready to move.

Two weeks later: One author's book is published. I've begun ghostwriting another's story. And the part that gets me every time? I didn't see it coming this way.

I thought the stories that would change everything would come from the big stages. From athletes. From celebrities. From CEOs or cultural icons. I assumed the breakthrough would come dressed in visibility.

But these stories? These came through quiet alignment. No fanfare. No lights. No curated moment. Just presence. Just purpose. Just truth.

What I realized is this: I didn't have to chase the stories that matter. They found me.

They weren't drawn in by performance. They were pulled in by resonance. By the clarity. By the stillness underneath the strategy.

These weren't high-profile voices. They were real people—with heart, with history, and with healing still in motion. And they didn't come because of branding. They came because of frequency.

Because that's the power of The Penthouse. It's not tied to fame. It's not limited to rooms with prestige. It's not about how many followers you have or who's watching.

It's a vibration. A decision. A rhythm of trust and obedience.

And when you operate at that level? You don't have to force breakthrough. Breakthrough finds you.

Penthouse Decoding:

Impact doesn't always arrive with a headline—it

moves through moments that feel ordinary.

Sometimes, the most transformative opportunities don't show up with noise. They don't come with applause or announcement. They unfold in silence. In stillness. In spaces where no one's watching but everything is shifting.

You may not know when it's going to happen. You might not recognize how it's going to unfold. But when you're operating in alignment, you don't need to chase the outcome. You simply honor the assignment—and trust that the right moments will rise to meet your presence.

What's meant for you rarely shows up loudly. It shows up faithfully. It meets you where you are— especially when you show up fully.

Reflection Point

• The moment you release control of the outcome, you make space for divine timing to move.

• Some of your most impactful moments will happen without a stage or spotlight.

• The people you're meant to serve won't be drawn to your performance—they'll be moved by your presence.

• You don't need to predict how something will happen. You just need to stay positioned for it.

Activation Cue

Where have you been expecting your breakthrough to show up in a specific way? What if it's already unfolding—but you've overlooked it because it wasn't loud? Reflect on the moments that felt small but led to unexpected alignment. Now, commit to showing up fully—even when there's no audience.

Chapter 6

The Convergence — When Paths Align Across Continents

There was a brief moment in Bangkok, Thailand, that didn't seem like much—until it was. I was seated in the VIP Lounge for speakers, finalizing last-minute details for my presentation at one of the largest fintech conferences in the world. It was one of those quiet pauses between movement and momentum.

Across from me at a large table sat another speaker from America. He was locked in on his laptop, focused and dialed in. He introduced himself and mentioned a design he had created for a global shoe company. I acknowledged it, but my mind was still adjusting to the time zone, the magnitude of the event, and the reality of how far I had come—geographically and personally.

Still, there was a quiet camaraderie between us. We were both far from home, seated in a space built for global voices, and though we didn't say much more, I understood his focus. I returned to my own screen, preparing for my moment on stage.

Other Americans were present as well—like the woman I sat with earlier, who spoke on multiple stages. It was a reminder: this conference may have been designed for the Asian market, but purpose had a global invitation list.

After Thailand, the momentum didn't stop.

I flew out, made my way to Green Bay for an in-person speaking engagement, and delivered a virtual webinar for an audience in Atlanta. From there, I returned the rental car I had driven to Wisconsin and boarded a plane to Central Florida. I decompressed after flying through multiple cities, countries, and two continents. And then, without pause, I drove from Central Florida to Miami.

All of it within a short window of time.

The work.
The speaking.
The movement.
The unfolding.

It was all happening with the same divine precision I've spoken of throughout this book.

When I arrived in Miami, I was there for a major conference that had been promoted widely across social media. It was expansive—held inside one of Miami's most glamorous hotel and conference centers, filled with people, brands, ideas, and opportunity.

Inside the larger experience was a branded mini-conference—one I had attended in Florida the year before. It didn't disappoint. The ambiance was vibrant, sociable, stylish. People were engaged. Conversations were alive. And the fashion statements were as bold as the ideas being exchanged.

I found a seat on the front row—at the end, where I could take it all in. I snapped a few photos and settled in to listen.

Then came a speaker who immediately caught my attention. He was the founder of a major tech innovation and now leading something new. He spoke about content, compensation, and how AI was shifting the entire landscape of advertising.

The panel was titled:
"AI Unlocking Advertising's Contextual Renaissance."

His thought process and delivery were magnetic. I was locked in.

When the panel ended and photos were taken, I walked up to introduce myself. He handed me his card and offered some feedback as we spoke— until suddenly, from behind me, I heard a voice:

"I was just with her in Thailand."

At first, I didn't register it. I was still immersed in the exchange. But then I heard it again:
Thailand.

I turned.

It was him.

The same speaker who had sat across from me in the Bangkok VIP Lounge just days earlier—working quietly at the same table. And now, here we were. Face-to-face again.

Same mission.
Different city.
Different country.
Different continent.

Let's pause there.

Because what are the odds?

This world is big.
Seven continents. Over 190 countries. Tens of thousands of conferences and business events happening every single week across the globe. The likelihood of two individuals—both traveling internationally, both committed to their craft, both flying through time zones—ending up in the exact same room twice within a week is astronomical.

We weren't in each other's networks.
We hadn't exchanged details or planned to meet again.
We were simply placed.

No algorithm. No invitation. No coordination.

Just two people who had answered the call of vision so clearly, so unapologetically, that alignment kept pulling us into the same orbit.

The magnitude of that didn't hit me right away. But later—when the crowd had thinned and the noise quieted—I sat with it.

You can't orchestrate this kind of timing.
You can't force this kind of flow.
This wasn't luck. It was evidence.
That something was working.
That movement was being mirrored.
That precision wasn't just a word I used—it was something I was living inside of.

I thought that was the end of the night.

But as I walked away—no expectations, no agenda
—
I was ushered into an unexpected space.

Not metaphorically. Literally.

No invitation. No push.
Just placement.
Just presence.
Just purpose.

Penthouse Decoding:

The Alignment Was Already in Motion. When paths cross more than once, across continents and circumstances, it's not coincidence—it's confirmation. Precision doesn't just guide where you go; it also reveals who's walking at the same pace, with the same calling. True alignment doesn't need a follow-up. It finds you again when you're already moving in purpose.

Reflection Point

• When paths cross more than once, across continents and circumstances, it's not coincidence —it's confirmation.

• Precision doesn't just guide where you go; it also reveals who's walking at the same pace, with the same calling.

• True alignment doesn't need a follow-up. It finds you again when you're already moving in purpose.

Activation Cue

Think back to a time when something or someone reappeared in your journey—unexpectedly. What confirmation did it bring? And how can you remain open to divine placement without needing control?

Chapter 7

The Valet, the Vibe, and the Vision — What Happens When You Show Up

I knew I needed to arrive a few minutes early. Something about this one felt different. The event was hosted inside a much larger global gathering during race car weekend in Miami Beach. But unlike the sprawling, often overwhelming crowds at these major conferences, this experience was intimate—deliberate. A curated space carved out for high-achieving, business-minded women to gather and breathe.

The energy was calm but electric. The venue was elevated, polished, and airy—an elegant contrast to the noisy excitement just blocks away. Shades of mauve and beige dressed the decor, and everything about it whispered intention. My car was valeted, and as I stepped out, I immediately felt it: something was about to happen.

And yet, I wasn't there to network. I didn't even want to talk. My plan was simple—take in the atmosphere, receive a little insight from the panels, and enjoy the ease of just being. I came in a breezy Miami Beach–inspired business casual look: linen pants, a structured blouse, and comfortable kitten heels. Everything about me said calm, open, and ready.

As I stood outside waiting for the doors to open, a few other women gathered nearby. One approached. Her demeanor was kind but curious. It was her first Female Quotient event and she didn't know what to expect. I smiled and told her, "You'll love it. You actually get to meet and talk to people here—like you're doing now."

We exchanged words, and somewhere in the conversation I mentioned that I publish books. That's when it happened—she reached into her bag and pulled out a book. The cover stopped me cold. A beautiful sepia-toned photograph of a Black woman from the 1800s stared back at me.

She explained that the book was about the first African-American female pilot—a woman whose legacy had been nearly forgotten. Her voice carried deep reverence as she talked about the historical figure's bravery, brilliance, and the desire to give her story the space it always deserved.

Then, almost shyly, I asked, "And what do you do?"

She paused before replying softly, "I'm a pilot."

It took me a moment to absorb that. The same legacy she was lifting up in this book lived within her. She had become the thing she admired—quietly, powerfully. She told me how her book had opened doors: red carpet invitations, celebrity conversations, speaking engagements. All for a story she wrote about someone else.

That's when I asked her the question that changed the air around us: "What about your story?"

She hesitated, then admitted she wanted to write it but didn't know how. She needed a guide, someone who could help her shape it. A ghostwriter. She had no idea that's exactly what I do.

We exchanged numbers.

She didn't walk like someone trying to be seen. She walked like someone who had already made peace with her power. I knew instantly she had a story the world needed—and it had nothing to do with who she admired. Her own life was a legacy in motion.

Inside the event, I sat through panel discussions on partnerships and leadership. The air was full of possibility. But the real connections were yet to come.

Standing in line for food, a woman behind me complimented my shoes. That simple exchange spiraled into something much deeper. She worked in PR—used to helping others shine. But recently, she felt the tug to move from behind the scenes to the front. She'd already started writing her story but felt stuck.

She said, "I think it's time to get from behind the desk."

I nearly laughed. Just weeks ago, I had said those exact same words.

I told her, "Here's what you do next," and laid it out step by step. Just like that.

Later in the same line, two more women struck up a conversation. We were all standing so closely it felt natural to join in. One asked what I did, and when I said I publish books and magazines, her eyes widened. "Wait, I just spoke at Money 20/20. Can I get your info?"

Then the other woman said she had been wanting to publish a magazine but didn't know how to start. Of course, that's what I do.

Three different women. Three different needs. One unexpected moment of alignment.

Whether they follow up or not isn't what matters.

What matters is what was happening through me, not just around me. The moment wasn't about marketing or pitching. It was about presence, clarity, and the magnetic power of purpose.

I had almost forgotten the event. It wasn't even on my radar until something internal nudged me. I got dressed, showed up, and let the moment unfold. I didn't chase a single opportunity. I simply walked into alignment—and alignment responded.

Penthouse Decoding: Alignment in Motion

1. Divine Alignment & Preparedness
You nearly missed this event. But a whisper of intuition told you to go. And when you did, you walked into a perfectly aligned moment. Not one conversation was forced. That's what happens when you're both prepared and in position.

2. Magnetism of Purpose
Your presence drew in the right people without effort. No pitch. No pressure. You spoke your truth, and it activated the very people who needed it.

3. Proof of Authority
You didn't lead with a resume. You just were who you are—and they saw it. That's true authority: when your value speaks before your credentials do.

4. Confirmation of Shift
The exact words you'd been saying—"get from behind the desk"—came back to you. This is confirmation. The shift is happening. You're stepping into greater visibility.

5. Next-Level Clarity

These weren't coincidences. These were reflections of your readiness. Your environment mirrored back your evolution. You were the resource in the room—and you didn't even have to try.

Reflection Point

- What moment confirmed your readiness without needing to prove it?

- Where have you shown up and been positioned without strategy?

- What does alignment feel like for you now—and how do you protect it?

Activation Cue

You don't need to chase validation. You are the confirmation.

Show up in truth, and the right people, places, and moments will recognize you before you even speak.

Chapter 8

This Wasn't the Greatest—For Me

―――――・―――――

I was standing at one of the most prestigious events in the world. The kind that creates millionaires, is owned by billionaires, shapes cultural waves, and turns global attention with a single post. The kind of event people dream about attending, much less being invited to. It is so powerful that my social media—stuck at 300 followers for what felt like years—suddenly surged to millions of views. I felt the shift. I saw the impact. And I respected it.

But even with the setting of this particular venue —sunshine, private beaches, and luxury all around me—something inside me wouldn't rest. Palm trees danced in the breeze, the elite moved freely, and conversations weren't just about wealth—they were about *the money being paid out*, the deals, the power moves, the financial flow. It wasn't just opulence; it was transactions at scale. And yet, even in the midst of it all, something in me stirred. It was exceptional—undeniably.

But it wasn't the greatest for me.

And that truth sat with me, pressed on me, and wouldn't let go.

I stood there in that atmosphere of wealth and access, and I knew—I was in brilliance, but not *my* brilliance. I wasn't being stretched. I wasn't being activated. I was visible, yes, but not fully seen. And that awareness hit harder than I expected.

That was the epiphany—the one that came before the journey I've described in these pages. Before the flights through cities, countries, and continents. Before the whirlwind of assignments and the stretch of divine alignment. This moment, right here in the midst of extravagance, quietly shifted everything.

Nearby stood someone I'd seen before—another familiar face from this global circle. We'd shared light conversations at events in different cities, and I knew him to be observant, grounded, wise. So I turned to him and spoke plainly:

"This is good, but I'm not using the full extent of what's in me. I'm on my way to speak at one of the largest fintech events in the world—this one's in Asia. Which is a light indication of what's in me…there's so much more - but I'm not using it."

As soon as I said it, something in me settled. Because it was the truth.

This was a high place—but it wasn't my highest.

Even as money surrounded me—physically, conversationally, energetically—I could feel that what I carried was built for more than presence. It was built for purpose. The kind of purpose that moves rooms, not just mingles in them. The kind that teaches, builds, stretches, and shifts ecosystems.

It was wild—this clarity arriving right in the middle of something most people would define as the pinnacle. But I couldn't un-feel it. I couldn't silence the knowing. I couldn't stay small in a space that didn't require all of me.

I knew I needed to press from goodness to greatness. I had already set it up—just days away. My next assignment wasn't a maybe. It was confirmation. I was already scheduled to speak at one of the largest fintech gatherings in the world. Asia was calling, and everything in me knew— that's where my real brilliance would meet the moment.

By the time I returned from Asia, I had elevated.

When I hit that stage at the global money and finance conference, I didn't just speak—I expanded. I moved in full clarity. That was my greatest. That was the space where things in me was required, welcomed, and released. It didn't just feel good. It felt right.

I will always honor where I stood when the realization came. It was luxurious, yes. Powerful. And beautiful in many ways. But it wasn't the top of the mountain for me.

I didn't want the best environment.
I wanted the best *me*.

And I didn't just find her—I became her.
On that stage, I showed up fully and placed myself there—on the world stage.
Not seeking approval, but answering the pressing within me to be seen, heard, and valued.

Penthouse Decoding:

The Greatest Was Waiting on the Other Side of Good

Some moments don't ask for a dramatic exit.
They ask for honest clarity in real time.
That's what happened to me.
I can still see myself standing there—surrounded by excellence, yet fully aware it wasn't the right kind of excellence for me.

And I'm just glad I said it out loud.
I'm glad I said it to someone else.
Because the moment I gave voice to the truth, the next level started moving in my direction.

Reflection Point

• Have you ever felt the difference between being present and being fully activated? It's subtle—until it isn't. That quiet ache when your voice is unused, your brilliance uncalled for, and your talent untouched? That's not discomfort. That's divine nudging.

• Good environments aren't always growth environments. Prestige doesn't always mean purpose. Just because it looks powerful doesn't mean it's the right container for your power.

• Sometimes your next level begins the moment you give yourself permission to want more. More meaning. More purpose. More alignment—not just applause or status.

• You don't have to feel guilty for wanting your "greatest." That desire isn't ego—it's evidence. Your next is calling, not because you're ungrateful, but because you're ready.

Activation Cue

Recall a moment when everything around you looked right—but something inside still whispered, "This isn't it."

- What was the environment?
- What did you feel in your body?
- What truth did you speak—or hold back?

Now ask yourself:

If I had stayed in that space, what brilliance in me would've gone untapped?

Chapter 9

When Elevation Activates Acceleration

There's a difference between going higher and going faster. For a long time, I thought they were the same. That if I was growing, things would naturally speed up. That if I was positioned well, movement would follow.

But now I know: Elevation and acceleration speak different languages.

Elevation is quiet.
It's the slow, intentional rising.
It's spiritual and steady.
You can feel yourself expanding—but you're still grounded.

Acceleration, on the other hand, is motion.
It's when everything you've been working on, believing for, preparing in silence—*suddenly starts moving*.
Faster. Louder. Sharper.

And the wild thing is, when acceleration hits, it doesn't ask for permission.
It doesn't knock.
It arrives with wind behind it.

And if you're not clear on who you are, it can feel like chaos instead of clarity.

I didn't realize I was in elevation until I had already been in it for years.
Those moments when I pulled back from noise.
When I focused on healing.
When I wrote books, mentored quietly, stood in rooms that stretched me—those were *elevation seasons*.

They felt personal. Internal.
There wasn't a lot of attention, but there was a *lot* of growth.
I was being built - stamina increased. Teaching me how to carry weight.
Not just responsibilities, but *reverence*.

I was being shaped.

But then… the shift came.

I didn't ask for it.
I didn't try to "manifest" it.
It just… arrived.

First in invitations I didn't expect.
Then in rooms I hadn't campaigned to be in.
Then in a sudden string of confirmations, clients, flights, and moments that moved fast.

Acceleration had found me.

And I felt it.
Not just in my schedule—but in my *spirit*.

The pace changed.
The rooms got bigger.
The clarity got louder.
And the distractions? They got cut quicker.

Because acceleration demands focus.

You can't move at this speed and carry what you used to.
Not emotionally. Not spiritually. Not relationally.

I remember looking at my calendar, trying to figure out how I had said "yes" to that many places, that many assignments, all in such a tight window.

Seven days.
Orlando. Chicago. Hong Kong. Thailand. Tokyo. Denver. Chicago again. Green Bay. Orlando. Then Miami.

That wasn't just movement.
That was *divine acceleration*.

And I knew it.

The way people found me.
The way opportunities opened without me chasing. The way my name was in rooms before I even arrived.

That's not strategy. That's speed.

Holy speed.
Momentum that doesn't make sense until you're *in* it.

But here's the thing about acceleration:

It's not about running.
It's about *responding*.

Responding to the window that's opened.
Responding to the trust placed in your hands.
Responding to the alignment that's been waiting for you to show up.

Elevation built my character.
Acceleration revealed my readiness.

You can't shortcut elevation.
And you can't slow-walk acceleration.
They serve different purposes—but together? They're powerful.

Because when you're elevated, you know who you are.
When you're accelerated, everyone else finds out, too.

And that's what I've been living.

I'm not just growing—I'm *moving*.

I'm being pulled into conversations I once dreamed about.

I'm being invited to share in places I used to observe.
I'm being recognized in spaces I didn't even try to enter.

But that didn't happen overnight.
That came after years of elevation—done in silence. In obedience. In refinement.

That's why I protect my energy differently now.
That's why I don't entertain what I used to.
I don't explain.
I don't rehearse.
I *respond.*

Because when acceleration comes, you don't have time to doubt.
You don't have time to perform.
You just have to be *ready.*

And I am.

There was a time I would've questioned whether I was qualified.
Now I understand that elevation already answered that question.

I don't move because I feel worthy.
I move because I've been *positioned.*

And I trust that positioning.

I've lived the climb.

Now, I'm living the *flight*.

And even though it's fast—*it's not out of control.*
It's precise.
Strategic.
Sacred.

There are still quiet moments.
Still pauses.
But even the silence is different now.
It's not empty—it's *full of momentum* that's gathering just beneath the surface.

And I've learned to respect that too.

So when people ask how I'm "doing all this"—how I'm managing to be in so many places, how I keep getting in the room, how I stay consistent...

I just smile.

Because they're seeing the *acceleration*.
But what they don't realize is, the *elevation* came first.

Penthouse Decoding:

Elevation raises your standard.
Acceleration raises your visibility.

Elevation happens in the dark.
Acceleration happens in the light.
But both are required.
One builds the foundation. The other reveals the structure.

When you've lived both, you don't panic at the pace.
You *trust the preparation.*

Reflection Point

- What have I built in private that's now creating public movement?

- Have I been resisting acceleration because I'm still trying to "feel ready"?

- Where do I need to embrace the speed instead of trying to slow it down?

Activation Cue

Stop mistaking speed for chaos.
This isn't out of control—it's in divine motion.
Move with it. You're ready.

Epilogue

The View from Here

I used to wonder what it would feel like to finally "arrive." To wake up one day and know that I had stepped into the life I was always meant to live.

But now I understand: arrival isn't a location—it's a rhythm.
And when you reach it, it's not loud. It's not flashy.
It's still. Full. Clear.

It looks like knowing.
It feels like peace.

It sounds like silence that doesn't scare you anymore.

Because when you've been in the climb, the view doesn't shock you.
It *settles* you.

You're not standing at the top thinking, *How did I get here?*
You're standing there saying, *I know exactly why I'm here.*

You remember the slow days.
You remember the pruning seasons.

You remember the rooms where your voice trembled but you spoke anyway.
You remember the long flights, the quiet drives, the silent assignments.

You remember who you had to release.
And how deeply you had to trust.

You didn't take the elevator up.
You climbed—step by step, choice by choice, chapter by chapter.

And now…
You can breathe.

Not because it's perfect.
But because it's *real*.

This view isn't about what you've accumulated.
It's about what you've *aligned* with.

There's nothing to prove here.
No spotlight needed.
No audience required.

This is the rhythm where peace becomes louder than applause.

Where clarity outruns competition.
Where stillness holds more power than performance.

This is where your presence speaks without effort.
Where your decisions feel light but firm.

Where your yes is sacred. And your no doesn't come with guilt.

This is where you start seeing the difference between attention and alignment.
Between being known and being *received*.

This is where you stop negotiating with rooms that weren't built for you.
Because now, you understand—you *are* the room.

You are the alignment.
You are the standard.
You are the one who changed.

And that's not pride.
That's power in its quietest, most honest form.

So no, I don't look around and ask "what's next" with fear.
I look around and say, *I'm ready*.

Ready to stay grounded while I grow.
Ready to let go of what no longer fits.
Ready to remain soft while standing strong.

The penthouse isn't about a skyline view.
It's about perspective.

And from here?

I see everything clearly.
The climb.
The shift.

The cost.
The reward.

And I see *me*—fully, finally, and freely.

Penthouse Decoding:

The highest level isn't loud. It's clear.

This view isn't a prize. It's proof.
That obedience works.
That alignment unfolds.
That you can grow without rushing, rise without explaining, and arrive without begging.

You didn't just make it.
You *matched it*.

Reflection Point

- How has the view changed now that I'm standing in alignment?

- What am I no longer willing to carry, even if it's familiar?

- What does peace look like now that I'm no longer trying to arrive?

Activation Cue

This is what it feels like to live aligned.
Breathe here.
Build here.
You've earned the view.

The Penthouse Decoding Companion
For the Aligned. The Elevated. The Ready.

::::::::::::

This companion is your quiet room at the top. No noise, no pressure—just the frequency of truth, ready for you to hear it. Use this section to revisit key themes and apply the blueprint beyond the page. You've read the stories. Now let's decode what they activated.

This isn't a recap. It's a realignment. This companion was created to distill the essence of *The Penthouse*—not chapter by chapter, but truth by truth. It draws out the patterns, frequencies, and principles that kept showing up in different environments, conversations, and moments of clarity. You've lived some of these lessons already. Others are still unfolding. Let this be your mirror, your guide, and your activation cue—again and again.

When You're Operating at the Next Level
• Reflection Point: In what ways are you already showing up as the future version of yourself?

• Activation Cue: Stop looking for the next level. Start stewarding the one you're already walking in.

The Room Will Recognize What's Been Refined

• Reflection Point: What parts of you were unseen until you elevated environments?

• Activation Cue: Your refinement doesn't require applause—it creates access.

Separation Is a Sacred Strategy

• Reflection Point: Who or what did you outgrow —and what did it teach you?

• Activation Cue: Disconnection isn't loss. It's alignment in motion.

Presence is a Currency

• Reflection Point: Where has your presence already made a way?

• Activation Cue: Don't shrink to fit proximity. Expand to match your precision.

Acceleration Isn't Hustle. It's Harmony.

• Reflection Point: What season are you in— elevation, acceleration, or both?

• Activation Cue: When flow meets focus, speed becomes sacred.

You Weren't Sent There by Accident

• Reflection Point: What moment confirmed you were right on time?

• Activation Cue: Divine timing doesn't ask permission. It positions.

The Imprint You Leave Is the Evidence You Were Aligned

• Reflection Point: What spaces felt different after you entered them?

• Activation Cue: Impact isn't always loud. Sometimes, it lingers in silence.

This Isn't Just a Book. It's a Mirror.

• Reflection Point: What truth did you see in these pages about yourself?

• Activation Cue: You didn't read this for information. You found recognition.

Intentional Elevation Is a Standard, Not a Season

• Reflection Point: How will you build this blueprint into your decisions?

• Activation Cue: You don't have to chase what's aligned. You just have to move like it's already yours.

This isn't the end of The Penthouse.

It's the beginning of your highest expression.

When you show up with clarity, you'll attract what matches your confidence.

When you lead with identity, the right doors open without a knock."

You were never chasing a lifestyle.

You were decoding your frequency.

About The Author

Vikki Jones is a global storyteller, visionary entrepreneur, and the award-winning founder and CEO of VMH Publishing, a hybrid publishing powerhouse known for producing content that inspires, educates, and leads. Through her innovative leadership, VMH has grown into a dynamic ecosystem that includes VMH Magazine, VMH Sports, and VMH Luxury+ Living, each serving as platforms for high-impact narratives across business, sports, culture, and wellness.

A prolific author and international speaker, Vikki has led the publishing journey of hundreds of writers while sharing her voice on stages around the world—from Thailand to Dubai—on topics ranging from digital innovation and storytelling to wellness and leadership. Her body of work, including *Trauma, The Power Within* and *The Penthouse*, reflects her commitment to truth-telling, healing, and intentional elevation.

Vikki's influence spans the media, tech, and sports industries, where she has moderated global conversations, covered America's greatest sporting events, and formed strategic alliances with major entities. She is also the creative force behind *The*

Penthouse podcast and luxury product collections that merge storytelling with lifestyle.

Driven by clarity, alignment, and vision, Vikki Jones continues to build platforms that unlock purpose, spotlight truth, and expand global reach —empowering others to rise with intention.